Introduction for Group Leaders

These advanced programs and exercises are designed to be used by adolescents in a group setting led by experienced group leaders. The instructions are written for teenagers and should provide enough information for leaders to guide the group through the exercises.

Some of the instructions refer to programs described in *The PRISM Workbook*. This original set of sixteen basic exercises provides a solid foundation in self-talk skills, communication skills, problem-solving skills, and relaxation skills, which should be helpful to teens using this new workbook.

Group leaders will find a more complete description of the program philosophy and specific instructions in *The Adolescent Self: Strategies for Self-management, Self-soothing, and Self-esteem in Adolescents.*

Introduction for Group Members

For those of you who are already familiar with PRISM, this workbook describes many new exercises that will help you feel even more "empowered." Here you get the chance to use your new ways of thinking, communicating, and problem-solving to deal with more challenging situations.

For those of you who are new to PRISM, it is important to understand the basic principles.

The purpose of this PRogram for Innovative Self-Management is to help you develop new skills in self-management. For those of you who do things under stress that you later regret (like using drugs or alcohol, getting into fights, hurting yourself, running away, stealing things, breaking things, saying things you don't mean, etc.), this program can help you develop better control over your behavior. For those of you who easily get depressed, angry, or anxious, self-management means developing better control over your thoughts and feelings.

Throughout these group sessions, you will learn the basic building blocks for self-management:

1. Self-Talk: You will gain more control over how you talk to yourself so you can have more control over your own feelings and reactions.

2. Self-Soothing: You will develop skills in how to calm your body down when you feel stressed or explosive. You will learn how to "slow time down."

3. Self-Expression (Assertiveness): You will learn how to let other people know what you are feeling and what you need in ways that are likely to work. You will learn to handle more and more challenging situations so that you end up feeling powerful rather than helpless.

Power is the main point here. We would like you to gain a sense of "empowerment," which is the ability to take charge and to not be a victim.

All of the techniques are designed to help you stop doing things automatically and to increase your abilities for personal choice. In PRISM, no one is trying to tell you what you should do. We are simply making sure that you are aware of all your options.

Contents

Introduction for Group Leaders   iii

Introduction for Group Members   v

GROUP 1. The Protective Shell*   1

GROUP 2. The Freeze-Frame*   3

GROUP 3. Dirty Fighting   6

GROUP 4. What Should You Do?   13

GROUP 5. Revising Personal History*   17

GROUP 6. Making It Clear   18

GROUP 7. Common "Bad" Messages   20

*Included in *The Adolescent Self: Strategies for Self-management, Self-soothing, and Self-esteem in Adolescents.*

GROUP 8. Losses   26

GROUP 9. Blasts from the Past   29

GROUP 10. Empathy Training*   30

GROUP 11. Discrimination Training*   31

GROUP 12. Modeling 1–2–3*   33

GROUP 13. Stress Inoculation*   34

GROUP 14. Jerk Therapy*   35

GROUP 15. Opposites Training*   36

GROUP 16. The Ally Contract*   38

GROUP 17. Accepting Criticism   41

GROUP 18. Giving Criticism   45

GROUP 19. Apologizing   47

GROUP 20. Say What You Mean and Mean What You Say   50

GROUP 21. The Five-Step Technique   52

GROUP 22. How to Talk to Girls/Boys   54

GROUP 23. Eleven Ways to Say "Hasta la Vista"   57

GROUP 1

The Protective Shell

In this group, you'll apply some of the skills you have been learning about self-talk.

First, someone in the group identifies self-talk that gets in the way. For instance, a girl may keep telling herself that "It's my fault that my father drinks and yells at me." Or maybe a boy tells himself over and over that "I always screw everything up!"

Next comes the dramatic part. Three group members (the group leaders can do this, too) stand on one side of the room. These are the "faulty self-talkers." The rest of the group gathers in front of a volunteer, faces the "faulty self-talkers," and forms a "protective shell" around the volunteer.

The "faulty self-talkers" start yelling all sorts of criticisms at the person, just like the thoughts that have been described. They try to move in and take over. The "protective shell" yells back with supportive comments, challenging the negative talk and defending the person.

The "faulty self-talkers" try to break through the shell (but please take it easy—this is only for fun). When the "protective shell" says things that are powerful, the "faulty self-talkers" have to back off and slink away.

If you are the person in the middle, just sit back and observe. Notice how similar this is to the fight that often goes on inside your head. After it is all over, discuss your thoughts and feelings and review some of the new strategies you may have learned from the "protective shell."

If there is time, the group leaders may teach you the "Protective Shell" visualization technique.

GROUP 2

The Freeze-Frame

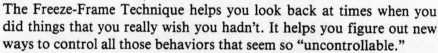

The Freeze-Frame Technique helps you look back at times when you did things that you really wish you hadn't. It helps you figure out new ways to control all those behaviors that seem so "uncontrollable."

Somebody in the group starts by picking out a situation, recent or long ago, that he/she now wishes could have been handled differently.

There are three things that have to happen for the Freeze-Frame to work. First, the person has to figure out what she was *trying* to do for herself with this behavior, even if it turned out miserably. Second, she needs to develop *self-respect* for the needs that she had at the time. Third, she must figure out *new ways* of handling those same needs in the future.

To do this, the person describes the situation leading up to the event, replaying it very clearly like watching a movie. Different group members can play different roles to make it more real. She should then start "slowing time down." As soon as she gets to the point just before she took drugs, ran away, cut her wrists, yelled at the teacher, etc., it is time to *freeze the frame.*

The group leader can now help the person identify the self-talk, the feelings, and the needs at this moment. The whole group can help with this. Remember that the needs and the feelings are okay—it's only the behaviors that she chose that caused problems.

3

Once the true needs are clear, it is time for everyone to help her figure out new ways that she could have taken care of these needs. Once you know the needs, you are smarter. Once you have new tools for handling the needs, you are more powerful.

The final step is to practice with the new behaviors and to get ready for the next time. Remember to keep asking yourself, "If I knew then what I know now, what might I have done?"

THE FREEZE-FRAME TECHNIQUE

Situation: Behavior:

Self-talk	Feelings	Needs	Options

GROUP 3

Dirty Fighting

Don't you get tired of learning how to be assertive? Isn't it a drag to always express yourself directly and respect the feelings of the other person? Don't you wish you could really let loose and be as mean and sadistic as possible to other people?

Dirty Fighting is for you. It's time that you received proper training in how to give low blows, avoid issues that other people want to discuss with you, and take advantage of people.

In this group, we first review the boring principles of Fair Fighting. Once that is out of the way, then we get to the fun stuff.

We will read through all the categories of Dirty Fighting, making sure that you each get a chance to practice and get even better at it than you already are. Finally, you will get something truly useful out of this program.

This group is fun and educational at all times, but the best day for this special session is April 1st.

6

FAIR FIGHT RULES

Ask for an Appointment for the Discussion.

1. Time
2. Place
3. How long?
4. What will you talk about?

Don't Hit "Below the Belt."

1. Don't call each other names.
2. Don't call each other's friends or family names.
3. Don't threaten, verbally or nonverbally.
4. Don't use violence.

 ### Use "I" Messages.

1. Example of "you" message: *"You always screw everything up."*

   a. Promotes defensiveness.
   b. Gives away power.
   c. Gives responsibility to the other person.

2. Example of "I" message: *"I feel really disappointed when you promise something but don't come through."*

   a. Reduces defensiveness.
   b. Retains control.
   c. Shows acceptance of responsibility.

Deal with Feelings First.

1. Express your feelings.   ·

    a. Become aware of what you are feeling.
    b. Label what you are feeling.
    c. Describe what you feel.

2. Listen.

    a. Be aware of what the other person is feeling by verbal and nonverbal cues.
    b. Label and check it out.
    c. Accept the other person's right to feel what he or she wants to feel.

Check It Out.

1. Words — verbal
2. Nonverbal cues
3. Thoughts and mind-reading

Ask for Specific Action.

1. Ask for what you want in detail.
2. Ask the other person what he or she wants, get details.
3. Compromise and negotiate.

Take a "Time Out" if Needed.

Use Teamwork.

1. Work Together to Use the Rules.

Never Give Up.

DIRTY FIGHTER'S INSTRUCTION MANUAL*

Setting the Proper Tone

Develop the ability to be hostile and mean or to throw temper tantrums and sulk for days when necessary. It is important also to learn the proper use of sarcasm and disapproving looks. Shouting and screaming are favorites, with threats thrown in for emphasis. Be sure to follow through with statements such as, "If I had known you'd get so upset, I wouldn't have brought it up in the first place," or "Obviously you can't control yourself, so there's no point in discussing it any further."

Developing the Proper Attitude

There are a number of situations that qualify you as being right and/or justified:

1. *Family wage-earner*—"I'm working to pay for it, so the discussion is over."
2. *Person in authority*—"That's the way things are. If you don't like it, that's just too bad. As long as you're here, you'll do what I tell you to do."
3. *Friend*—"I wouldn't think of bothering you unless I really needed your help. I'll really be hurt if you refuse."
4. *Girlfriend/Boyfriend*—"I shouldn't have to ask you to do things for me. You should know how I feel without my having to tell you."
5. *Parent (with children)*—"I'm your father (or mother) and I know what's best for you."

The Importance of Good Timing

Begin an argument just before your father leaves for work. Bother your parents with something you want from them just as they sit down to watch their favorite TV program. In general, keep in mind that it is

---

*Adapted from *The Dirty Fighter's Instruction Manual*, by Alan Summers, Transactional Dynamics Institute, Glenside, PA.

best to attack others when their guard is down, when they least expect it, or when they are least able to defend themselves.

Collect Injustices

Let your anger build up to the point where you explode over relatively minor issues. Then, when you've had enough, shout, scream, terrorize, even hit. You will be surprised to learn how good it feels to get things off your chest.

Help When People Don't Want It

There are many chances to give advice, tell people what they should do, how they should feel, what they should think. It doesn't matter whether or not they have asked your opinion: Go right ahead and give others the benefit of your experience. You know what's best!

Don't Get Mad, Get Even

Anger expressed openly can be uncomfortable for all concerned, so learn to find other ways to channel your feelings. Get revenge by sulking, cheating on your girlfriend or boyfriend, spending someone else's money, talking behind someone's back, etc. In general, it is always a good idea to find ways to screw up the other person's confidence or independence.

Play Psychiatrist

Analyze others, point out their shortcomings, their hang-ups and, where possible, explain in psychological terms the weaknesses you see in their character. Example: "You have a mother complex," or "The reason you say that is because you're basically insecure." The real secret in playing psychiatrist, however, involves the skillful use of labels. For instance, you may reveal to someone they are a "hopeless paranoid," "an egomaniac," or a "dominating bitch." You can find a label for any behavior you don't like. By the way, if they object to your evaluation it is undoubtably because they have an "inferiority complex" or they "can't face the truth."

Wipe Someone Out with Humor

Be sarcastic, but always smile to show that it's all in good fun. If the other person begins to get defensive, you can accuse him or her of being overly sensitive.

Play One Person Against the Other

When out with a friend of the opposite sex, always take long looks at passing strangers of the opposite sex. Compare the success of others to those of the person you are with. A parent should never miss a chance to hold up the accomplishments of one child to another. A child should likewise never miss an opportunity to play one parent against the other.

Play the Martyr

Go out of your way to give up your needs for others, even to the point of letting others take advantage of you. Later, when you want to get your way, you can make statements like: "How could you do this to me? After all the things I've done for you," or "See how I've suffered because of you."

Never Back Down

Backing down can only be considered by the opposition as a sign of weakness.

Never Accept an Apology

Never let the other person think that they are forgiven. How else will they remember the next time? Learn to hold grudges, for years if necessary.

Put the Other Person in a Double Bind

Criticize your girlfriend/boyfriend for gaining a little weight, not keeping up his/her appearance and the like. Then, when she/he dresses up and looks especially good for a party, accuse her/him of trying to impress people or flirting. Parents should hound their children about hanging around the house too much. Then, when they are getting ready to go out to play, they should remind them of some chore they were supposed to do or tell them it's too close to supper.

The Kitchen Sink Technique

Throw everything into the argument but the kitchen sink. No need to stick to the issue at hand; now is the time to bring up all the other incidents that have been bothering you. Talk about his or her past failings, defects in his or her character, etc. Before long, so many issues will have been brought up that the other person will feel that winning an argument with you is impossible.

Ambush — The Art of Getting the Other Person into a Corner

Be on the lookout for situations you can use later. Go through your boyfriend's wallet, listen in on the telephone extension, quiz your parents' friends to dig up dirt about them. You will be amazed to find how much ammunition you can gather for your next fight. Once you have become good at this, others will think twice about bringing up even the most reasonable complaint.

GROUP 4

What Should You Do?*

This group is designed to get you thinking. Every day, we each try to decide what is right and what is wrong. Sometimes the decisions are very easy, but most of the time the decisions are very complicated.

You might have a rule about keeping secrets. If a friend told you that he had a crush on a girl but asked you not to tell anyone, you would probably honor his request. But if the same friend told you he was planning to kill himself, you might decide that keeping the secret was not as important as trying to save his life.

These "shades of gray" happen all the time. Today, we will describe different situations that offer tough choices about values and morals. See if you can be as honest as possible in discussing what you would do and why.

*Thanks to Jane Wells, Ph.D., for this technique.

13

DILEMMAS

Dilemma #1

Late one night, Dave (16) and Tom (13) take Tom's mother's new Trans Am out for a ride while she is asleep. During their ride, they accidentally hit a parked car and, in the excitement, just take off. They get home, park the car where they found it, and put the keys back, hoping Tom's mother would think someone hit it during the night.

- Should they tell her?
- Should they wait to see what happens?
- What about the car they hit?
- What if someone were hurt?
- What would be the right thing to do?

Dilemma #2

Dave is planning to work in construction. He likes to be outside and wants to make some good money. He gets a chance to work with his uncle and some of his cousins who have a business. David is not very strong, and the job is tough on him. He's afraid to say anything to his uncle because of the closeness of the family. He doesn't think it's going to work out, because he can't physically do the job.

- What should he do?
- What's the problem?

Dilemma #3

Tommy (18) is thinking about getting married to Suzanne (17) who he has known for about a year. Their parents are not in favor of the idea, because they believe they're both too young. Tommy and Suzanne are thinking about running away together because they want to do it in spite of their families' opposition.

- Should they run away together to get married?
- Should they talk to their parents?

- What should they say?
- Have you been or known someone in this situation?
- How would you handle it?
- What would be important things to think about?

Dilemma #4

Kevin's dad drinks a lot, and when Kevin gets home his dad some-times yells at him and hits him. Kevin thinks he does this for no reason. It's getting worse, and Kevin's really getting bothered. You're Kevin's friend and don't know what to do, but know that you'd like to help him out if you can. You're thinking of telling someone, but you know Kevin doesn't want you to do anything.

- Should you try to say something?
- Who would you tell?
- What would you say?
- Should you just forget it?
- Have you or anyone you know been in this situation?
- What's the right thing to do?
- When isn't it right for a parent to hit a child? When is it?

Dilemma #5

Carlos' girlfriend, Theresa, is attacked and raped one night on her way home from the store where she works. Carlos was supposed to pick her up, but couldn't because his car broke down. When he found out what happened later that night, he got very upset and angry.

- What was Carlos feeling?
- What kind of girl is Carlos' girlfriend?
- What was Theresa feeling?
- What would you have done?
- Has that happened to you or anyone you know?
- What should Carlos do now?

Dilemma #6

Hector's girlfriend, Tina, is pregnant. Hector feels he's not ready to be a father and doesn't like the way things have been. They've been arguing a lot. Hector thinks she's just using this against him, so he's stayed away. Tina wants to see Hector but he refuses and won't talk to her.

- What is Hector feeling?
- What is Tina feeling?
- What should he do?
- What should she do?
- Should she live at home?
- Should she have the baby?
- Should a child not have a father?
- Should Hector offer to get married?

GROUP 5

Revising Personal History

Everybody makes decisions about themselves, or about how the world works, after important events.

For example, a boy watches his mother getting hit by his father, and he is afraid to do anything. His self-talk is, "I am weak and girls can never respect me." Another example: A girl decides not to have sex with her boyfriend. Her self-talk is, "I am only attractive to men if I am sexual with them." The opposite example: A girl goes to bed with a guy even though she doesn't want to, and he becomes cold and rejecting afterwards. Her self talk is, "There is something wrong with me."

You all know enough about self-talk at this point to realize that *negative self-talk can really screw things up*. Even though bad things happen, the worst damage often comes from how we blame ourselves or mistrust others as a result.

In the Revising Personal History exercise, someone will pick out a situation like this, and the group will help him or her act it out. Then, we will zero in on the self-talk and see if there are some different conclusions that might help. We have to keep asking the question: If you knew then what you know now, what new self-talk might you have used?

17

GROUP 6

Making It Clear

Most people have had at least one experience when someone else did something or said something that had a very destructive effect. This technique is designed to help correct the damage that was done in the past. This works when someone is still being affected by something that was said or done in the past.

Someone starts by volunteering a situation. The group leader will then help you imagine that the person from the past has decided to join us in the group to straighten out some of the things that he said or did back then. With her eyes closed, the volunteer will imagine that the door is opening and the person from the past comes and sits down in the room. The group leader will play the role of this other person.

This person from the past has some things to say that he was not aware of or could not say back then. The role of the volunteer is to sit back and take in the new information.

Here is what the person will say:

1. Identify what he has done. ("I realize now that I turned away from you when I married your stepmother.")
2. Explain that it was not consciously meant to hurt. ("I had no idea of how deeply that would hurt you.")

3. Take full responsibility. ("The reason I did this was because of my own insecurity in my new marriage, *not* because something was really wrong with you.")
4. Express remorse. ("If I had known then what I know now, I never would have let my needs get in the way of being a good father to you — I'm sorry.")
5. Give permission to be angry or unforgiving. ("I'm not saying this so you'll forgive me — I just want to relieve you of some of the burden you've carried.")

It doesn't matter whether this person would really say this now. What matters is that the volunteer is able to feel less responsible for what was said or done back then.

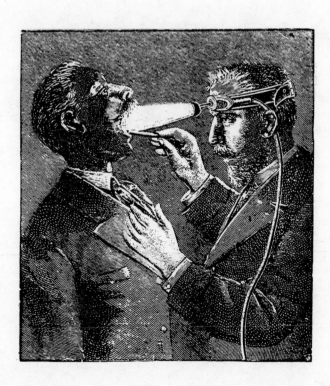

GROUP 7

Common "Bad" Messages

Parents and other adults who are important to you often make the mistake of sending the message that there is something seriously "wrong" with you. This is different from correcting wrong behavior — that's a parent's important job. Instead, these "bad" messages tell you that there is something really wrong with *you*.

On the handout that follows, you will see examples of the most common messages that kids are "bad." See which ones sound familiar to you and notice your reactions. Do you feel like protesting? Do you secretly believe the messages are true? Are you able to ignore them?

The more you understand about these messages, the more capable you will be of dealing with them. Let the group help you prepare self-talk, which can talk back to these "bad" messages.

COMMON "BAD" MESSAGES*

Here are some of the bad messages you may have received as a child. If you find one or more statements that sound familiar—or if some of these messages make you think, "That's no bad message, that's reality!"—you have probably internalized those negative messages.

"You're Unlovable" Messages

- "I hate you."
- "I wish you were dead."
- "Get out of my life."
- "I'm sorry you were ever born."
- "You're no good."
- "You're just like your mother, a heartless, faithless whore."
- "You're just like your father, a mean, irresponsible bastard."

ACTION: Cruel, insensitive, or neglectful treatment

"Don't Trust Others" Messages

- "Most people will screw you in a minute if you give them half a chance."
- "If you want it done right, do it yourself."

ACTION: Parent repeatedly promises to come to a graduation, a big football game, etc., but fails to show up.

*Taken from *Imaginary Crimes*, L. Engel & T. Ferguson (1990), Boston, MA: Houghton Mifflin.

Sex Role Messages

- "Medical school is too hard for a girl. Be a nurse instead."
- "Having a career and being a mother just don't mix."
- "You'll never find a husband if you are too independent, too outspoken, or too smart."
- "Your brother will have to support a family someday, so we'll send him to college."
- "Big boys don't cry."

ACTION: A father encourages his son, but not his daughter, to plan a college career. A mother encourages her daughter, but not her son, to share vulnerable feelings.

"You're Incompetent" Messages

- "Why can't you ever do anything right?"
- "You're so lazy and undisciplined you'll never amount to anything."
- "You're all thumbs."
- "You always find some way to screw up."

ACTION: Constant criticism

"You're Crazy" Messages

- "You're just like your Uncle Jake [an alcoholic or hospitalized mental patient]."
- "You're nuts. You've always been nuts and you'll always be nuts."
- "Nothing's wrong with Daddy. Daddy's just not feeling well. But don't you dare mention this to anybody or Daddy will lose his job and we'll starve" [when a parent is drunk].

ACTION: A parent denies incest, violence, or verbal abuse.

"You Can't Trust the Opposite Sex" Messages

- "Men only want one thing—sex. And once they get it they'll dump you."
- "Women only want one thing—a meal ticket. A free ride. Once they get it, they will tie you down and henpeck you to death."
- "You can't deal with a man directly. You have to learn to manipulate him."
- "You can't ever let a woman know you really care about her. If you do she'll manipulate and control you."
- "Men are bastards, but you can't get by without them."

ACTION: Complaining constantly to a child about a spouse

"Succeeding Is Failing" Messages

- "The only way to get to the top is over the dead bodies of those on the bottom."
- "Money is the root of all evil."
- "It is easier for a camel to pass through the eye of a needle than for a rich man to enter the kingdom of heaven."

ACTION: Criticizing anyone who is wealthy, successful, or famous

"It's Dangerous to Criticize" Messages

- "If you can't say something nice, don't say anything at all."
- "You'll destroy your mother if you imply she's got a drinking problem."

ACTION: A mother cries in her room for hours after her teenage daughter criticizes her.

"Don't Grow Up" Messages

- "You children are the only thing that gives my life meaning."
- "There's only one right way to do things, and that's my way."
- "You'll always be Daddy's [or Mommy's] little girl."

ACTION: Stepping in to take over instead of letting the child learn to solve her own problems

ACTION: Disapproving of a teenage child's attempts to date; not letting a teenager date until much later than is customary in their community

"Pleasure Is Dangerous" Messages

- "Idle hands are a devil's playground."
- "Masturbation will drive you insane."
- "Sex is nasty."
- "Sex will make you burn in hell."
- "Sex is only pleasurable for men. For women it is something to be endured."

ACTION: Acting uptight whenever anyone else is having fun

"Don't Let Yourself Relax" Messages

- "If things seem good, disaster lies just around the corner."
- "Knock on wood [i.e., if you dare to say that things are good, they will surely go bad]!"
- "Don't be so cocky and full of yourself."
- "If you've finished today's homework you'd better start on to-morrow's."

ACTION: Never relaxing

"Don't Take Care of Yourself" Messages

- "Be sure everyone else is taken care of before you serve your-self."
- "Don't be so selfish and self-indulgent."
- "You'd best stay away from doctors: if you're feeling bad the best thing to do is to ignore your symptoms and work right through it."

ACTION: Parent refuses to let child stay home from school when ill.

ACTION: Parent refuses to obtain necessary medical or dental care.

Martyr Messages

- "I had a very difficult delivery and almost died when you were born."
- "I gave up a promising career [on stage, in business, as an artist, etc.] to take care of you."
- "You're my cross to bear. You always were."
- "I stayed with a monster for all these years for your sake."
- "Why do you make me suffer so?"

ACTION: Never taking care of oneself, sighs, sad looks

GROUP 8

Losses*

Loss is hard to deal with. For everybody. Losing something or someone means you have to change. You have to change to adjust to the absence of the person or the thing that used to be there. And you have to get used to something new. Plus, you probably really miss the way it used to be. Loss also causes a lot of stress, depending on what it is. When a parent or sibling dies, that kind of loss is probably greater than losing your first job.

There are stages that we all go through when we lose something or someone important to us. It's okay—and even good—to go through these stages. It's normal. But if we get stuck in any stage and stay there for a long time, that's not good.

The stages we all go through when we lose something are Denial, Anger, Depression, Grief, and Acceptance. Examples of the self-talk you might hear at each stage are listed on the handout: (Notice how the self-talk gets increasingly more positive and realistic with each stage.)

*Thanks to Jane Wells, Ph.D., for this technique.

LOSS STAGES

Denial

- "She hasn't left — she's just on an extended home pass."
- "My dog didn't die — he simply ran away from home."
- "I'm not leaving this program. What discharge date? What are you talking about?"

Anger

- "I am really mad at my Dad for dying. How could he do that to me?"
- "How dare she leave this place and leave me here!"
- "I am so mad that he left our group and went on without me. We were going to do lots of things together."

Depression

- "I don't think I can go on anymore since my friend died."
- "It's not worth living since my mother left."
- "I don't want to be here anymore since she left our group; it makes me too sad."

Grief

- "It's really sad and unfair that my friend had to die."
- "I miss the way it used to be when my friends were here."
- "I feel like I am mourning for my grandfather who has died."

Acceptance

- "I miss my Mom, but I know that I can deal with it."
- "I don't like it at all that my dog died, but I can't change it now."
- "I miss my friends since they left our school, but I'm glad for them and one day, I'll leave, too."

GROUP 9

Blasts From the Past

This group helps you see, very clearly, the progress you have made in taking charge of your own behavior.

Most of us forget how much we have changed. It's easy to get discouraged when things are not going well and to think that things are just the way they used to be.

Blasts from the Past means that someone describes a situation from the past when he/she really blew it. Usually it makes sense to choose an incident around the time when you were first brought into treatment.

This person now role-plays this event with the help of the group. Here's your chance to act (temporarily) just the way you used to! Describe the self-talk each step of the way, and then react in the explosive, negative, or destructive way that you used to.

Now replay the same tough situations as if it were taking place in the present. Maybe the same tough situation does keep happening, like parents treating you in ways that you don't like. Pay attention to the self-talk and the ways you handle (or would handle) this same event now. Pay attention to everything that is different from the past: self-talk, emotional reactions, communication skills, new ways of dealing with it, etc.

When you forget how far you've come, try this again.

GROUP 10

Empathy Training

Empathy Training is an advanced form of Active Listening (see *The PRISM Workbook*).

This works especially well in family therapy or in group therapy when there is a conflict between two people. It can also work when you are having a conflict with someone outside the group—you can role-play it in the group.

For example, a girl is furious with her father for remarrying and not having enough time and attention for her. The girl needs to describe this situation in detail to the group.

The next step is for the girl to play the role of her father. She should try to sit like him, talk like him, and especially think like him. She then describes what he thinks and how he feels about this whole thing.

She has to really play this role from the father's point of view. It doesn't matter whether she agrees or approves. The goal is simply to "get it" from his side.

The group keeps giving her feedback about how well she is doing.

Maybe she is not seeing some of his feelings or his reasons for doing what he is doing. The group needs to keep challenging her until she gets it right.

If two group members are having a conflict, they simply play the role of each other, also trying it again and again until they get it just right.

The goal here is not problem-solving, but simply understanding. Often the solutions are easier when you get a clearer picture of where the other person is coming from.

GROUP 11

Discrimination Training

Discrimination is the ability to tell the difference between things. A great baseball hitter can discriminate between a fastball and a curveball. A first grader learning to read begins to discriminate between "b" and "d" or "O" and "Q." In the middle of the night, a mother can discriminate her baby daughter's little cry from all the other sounds she may be hearing. This is a very important skill.

Most of us, however, have certain areas in which we don't discriminate very well. A boy who becomes extremely mistrustful around authority figures may be thinking, "Because my father was mean and unfair, all authority figures will be mean and unfair." This sounds very much like "Black and White" thinking (see *The PRISM Workbook*).

Your group leader will explain to you about Pavlov and his dogs, plus the story of Little Albert. (To group leaders: Give a brief description of negative classical conditioning. Explain how negative associations can develop and generalize.) This will demonstrate the way we become conditioned to certain cues and how difficult it can be to change that.

In the group session, someone needs to volunteer a situation in which he keeps reacting in an old way. For example: A boy was once told by his girlfriend, "I need to talk to you." It turned out that this was a

31

conversation in which she broke up with him, which crushed him. Now, whenever any other girl he is dating says that she needs to talk to him, he becomes panicky and angry. Because he's so upset, he starts acting rude and actually gets her mad at him. In this case, he is not able to discriminate between the old girlfriend's words and other people using the same words but possibly meaning something very different.

Another example would be the girl whose father used to get drunk and physically attack her older brother, while she looked on helplessly. She felt so helpless that she would cut herself. She remembers the signs that this was about to happen: tension, raised voices, etc. Now, whenever she feels any tension or conflict between teachers (authority figures like dad) and male peers (like her brother), she gets the same feelings and starts to cut herself. This is true even though the situations are different: The incidents do not lead to violence, the teacher is not out to humiliate the boy, nobody is drunk, etc.

The group leader will draw a chart on the board, comparing the old situation with the new one. You will list the ways in which the old and the new are the same—and then list all the ways in which they are different. This part is Discrimination Training. With the help of the group, the volunteer will learn to spot signs that are truly danger signs, and also spot the signs that tell him/her that the old situation is different from the new one.

Modeling 1-2-3

One of the best ways to learn how to do something new is by *modeling*: watching someone else do it first. Many athletes have learned to use this all the time. Research has shown that this is a way of programming your brain — while you are in charge:

Someone in the group should pick out a behavior that he would like to do better. For example, someone might choose asking a girl out for a date. He would try the following *modeling* steps:

1. Close your eyes and imagine someone really cool and sophisticated asking a girl out. This should be someone who seems very different from you: It seems really easy for him, and he is successful. Observe very carefully and take it in.
2. Now imagine someone similar to you doing the same thing. This guy isn't quite as smooth about it, but he still is able to do it.
3. Now imagine yourself trying it. It may not be easy, and it may not be perfect — but you can still imagine yourself doing it "good enough." See if you can use some of what you have observed and felt with the other models.

After this example, each of you can try the same thing. See if you can carry around the model image like an "ally" in future situations.

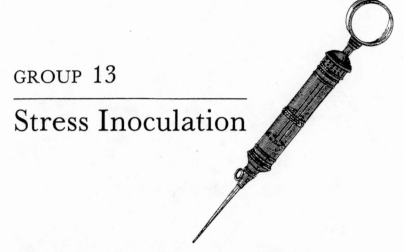

GROUP 13

Stress Inoculation

This technique uses self-talk to help you deal with something that you *know* is going to be tough for you.

The best times to use Stress Inoculation is when you feel anger, fear, or pain. For example, a teenage girl may be preparing to enter a really difficult family counseling session. She is afraid, based on past experience, that her father will say something that will make her blow up. This time, she wants to handle it differently.

She needs to find four different sentences of self-talk. Each one relates to a different stage:

1. **READY** (the day before):
"I will be powerful if I *don't* let my father get to me!"
2. **SET** (just as it starts):
"Okay, it's about to start — get ready for the jolt!"
3. **GO** (it's happening):
"He's doing it. Hang in there! You can handle this!"
4. **AFTER** (after it's over):
"Okay, good job — I knew you could do it!"

or

"Okay, you tried, but it didn't work — what can you learn from this for next time?"

Practice this in group, with different people taking turns. Write down your four sentences and rehearse them as the event gets closer. See if you can really use them.

GROUP 14

Jerk Therapy*

Jerk Therapy is a fancy name for a self-talk strategy. It involves explaining an old situation in a new way.

Think of someone who really causes you trouble. You just cannot get along with this person, and he/she always seems to irritate you. The first step is to try and work out your differences and improve communication. But, if this is not possible (which is often true), then it's time for Jerk Therapy.

When it seems that somebody is treating you unfairly, you are still in charge of how you react. Picture a big chart with lines across it at the top (100%), a little ways down (80%), and most of the way down (20%).

The perfect friend or ally gives you 100% of what you need. Even someone who gives 80% is probably a terrific friend. With the person who is upsetting you, you need to make a decision that you will not react until he/she crosses the bottom line: 20%.

The challenge with Jerk Therapy is to adjust your expectations and not let this other person have any power over you. However, if the other person's behavior becomes too insulting or intolerable (below 20%), you *must* react.

Try putting different people on the chart and figure out at what percent they land. Practice Jerk Therapy so that you are still in charge.

*Thanks to Gene Morris, Ph.D., for this technique.

GROUP 15

Opposites Training*

Opposites Training is an easy strategy for changing your thoughts, feelings, and behavior. It doesn't always work, but it's a good tool to carry around with you for a lot of situations.

Opposites Training works because it is impossible to do two opposite things at the same time. You can't be relaxed and tense at the same moment. You can't be putting your fist through a wall at the same time that you are touching something gently.

The goal here is to figure out some opposite thing that you can do or say to yourself when you're starting to lose it. Here are some examples:

1. Putting fist through door. *Opposite—hold palms open so they can't make a fist.*
2. Tensing muscles. *Opposite—deep breaths and let yourself "flop".*
3. Reaching for a cigarette. *Opposite—sit on your hands.*

*Thanks to Jim Zians, M.A., for this technique.

4. Yelling at someone. *Opposite — whisper.*
5. Feeling tense inside. *Opposite — say the word "calm" over and over.*

6. Tempted to hit someone. *Opposite — touch something very gently.*
7. Withdrawing from others. *Opposite — make an effort to say something.*

You can probably think of many more examples. By the end of the group, each person should identify and rehearse the "opposites" plan.

GROUP 16

The Ally Contract

Sometimes it is very hard to change a behavior just by yourself. Most of us need some help from an "ally" to stay on track.

The Ally Contract helps each of you set up a plan for specific behavior change with the help of an "ally." The steps are very simple:

1. First, you *identify the behavior* you want to change.
2. Then you *pick someone* in your life who can help you notice this behavior.
3. Together, you *decide on a signal* that this person can give you when they catch you doing it.
4. You need to *let the other person know* that you received the signal and that you appreciate the help.
5. Finally, you need to make sure and *use some positive self-talk* about your ability to take charge.

Let's say a boy wants to stop cursing so much. He may ask his girlfriend to be his "ally." Whenever she notices him starting to curse, she can quietly go over to him and hold his hand, or maybe she could wink at him from across the room. If he has asked for her help, he will

THE "ALLY" CONTRACT

Each of us needs help from time to time in changing daily behaviors, like eating too fast, interrupting others, nailbiting, mumbling, putting yourself down, etc. This worksheet is designed to help you turn a friend into an "ally" who can remind you when you slip into the old habit. Since you are asking your "ally" for help, their reminders will be gifts to you rather than nagging.

Target Behavior	Ally	Feedback from Ally	Feedback to Ally	Feedback to Self

feel like she is supporting him and not nagging him. He then needs to give her a signal back to say, "Thanks for the reminder." Next, he needs to tell himself something like, "I'm glad I can be in control of what I say!" All of this needs to be agreed upon in advance.

Most people turn out to be very good "allies" when you ask for their help in the right way. Just make sure that you show your appreciation for their help, rather than acting resentful as if they're trying to control you. You can set up an Ally Contract with someone in the group or make a plan involving someone else whom you trust.

GROUP 17

Accepting Criticism

Accepting Criticism is very difficult for most teenagers. That's why we have a special group so you can learn new ways to handle it.

Some criticism is totally unfair, and other criticism may be justified. Either way, it helps to "play detective" and find out what the other person is truly upset about. If there is some valuable feedback in the criticism, then you can learn from it. If not, then you can just shrug it off.

The steps here are similar to what you have learned before about responding to teasing and resisting peer pressure (see *The PRISM Workbook*). First, you make sure that your nonverbal message is clear and assertive. Then you make sure to listen, ask questions, respond clearly, and use positive self-talk throughout.

Follow the steps in the next few pages. Use your own situations or practice with the role-plays.

ACCEPTING CRITICISM*

It's important to think of accepting criticism as an act of maturity, rather than the act of a wimp. We emphasize that this approach only applies when someone is offering criticism in a halfway reasonable manner. If the criticizer is being too aggressive or insulting, another strategy is needed, like "time out."

How to Look and Act:

1. Face the person.
2. Make eye contact.
3. Use a serious voice and serious facial expression.
4. Keep a straight body posture.

You want to make sure to communicate to the other person that you are taking what he/she has to say seriously. If you look away or clown around or slouch, the other person won't know that. The more the other person feels respected, the less likely that the situation will turn into a bigger conflict. Think of it this way: If you were telling someone something that upset you, wouldn't you want to be taken seriously?

What to Say:

1. Listen to the person.
2. Ask the person to explain, if you don't understand.
3. Apologize. Let the person know that you're sorry for what happened.
4. Tell your side of the story so the person knows how the mistake happened. You still want to make sure that you're taking responsibility for what you did or failed to do.
5. Ask for ideas about how to handle this better.

*Adapted from J. B. Schumacher et al. (1988). *Social skills for daily living*, Circle Pines, MN: American Guidance Service.

6. Agree with the criticism or let the other person know that the feedback is valuable to you.
7. Let the person know that you will try and handle this better in the future.

Role-Plays:

Role-play situations are then introduced to practice this. The instructions are all for the person who is doing the criticizing—the one criticized is left with the task of responding in a way that follows the principles in the outline. Remember that this is not always the best way to respond, but rather one more option:

1. You and your partner work together in a restaurant. You are angry because your partner agreed to work for you yesterday, but never showed up.

   • "So where were you yesterday?"
   • If asked to explain, say: "You said that you'd work for me, but you never showed up!"
   • If asked for ideas about how to change this in the future, say: "Next time if you're not going to be able to make it, let me know or get someone to take your place."

2. Your partner is your roommate. You are angry because your partner wore your clothes without asking you.

   • "You've done it again!"
   • If asked to explain, say: "You wore my best shirt, and now it's dirty. I don't have anything to wear tonight."
   • If asked for ideas about how to handle this next time, say: "Next time, ask me before you borrow my clothes."

3. You are your partner's boss at a clothing store. You are angry because your partner has worn blue jeans to work because her other clothes were dirty.

- "That does it! Either clean up your act or find a new job!"
- If asked to explain, say: "I told you to wear dress clothes to work. You've ignored that rule twice now."
- If asked for ideas on how to deal with this problem, say: "You have to figure out what you're going to wear at the beginning of each week and plan it out."

4. You are the parent of your teenage partner. You are really upset because your son or daughter borrowed the car and didn't return it in time.

- "That does it! No more driving for you!"
- If asked to explain, say: "I told you I needed the car back by 6:00 and you're really late. Now it's too late for me to make it to my meeting."
- If asked for suggestions, say: "Next time ask me when I need the car back so you'll know before you take it."

GROUP 18

Giving Criticism

Like accepting criticism, most people are not very good at Giving Criticism. It's easy to come on too strong (aggressive) or to back off and not say enough (passive).

The steps in this exercise teach you how to present your criticism assertively. Like with other assertiveness approaches, the goal is to get your point across in such a way that the other person can hear you and feel respected. Remember to be as specific as possible.

GIVING CRITICISM*

1. Only suggest realistic changes.
2. Only suggest one thing at a time.
3. Do *not* put down the other person.
4. Stay calm; if you get angry and agitated, you have lost your power.
5. Be prepared to admit that you might have made a mistake.

*Adapted from J. B. Schumacher et al. (1988). *Social skills for daily living*, Circle Pines, MN: American Guidance Service.

Steps: Nonverbal

1. Face the person.
2. Make eye contact.
3. Keep a serious voice and expression.
4. Keep a straight body posture.

Steps: Verbal

1. Ask the person if you can talk.
2. Tell the person how you feel about what he/she has said or done. Remember to make "I feel" statements about a *specific* behavior.
3. Give the person a reason for changing.
4. Ask if the person understands.
5. Explain again, if needed. Be prepared to use the Special Strategies you have learned: Broken Record, State the Importance, Admitting Past Errors, etc. (see *The PRISM Workbook*).
6. Ask to hear the other person's side or feelings.
7. Suggest how the other person might change this.
8. Thank the person for listening.
9. Change the subject so the relationship can feel "normal" again.

Suggested Situations:

1. Use situations from your own experience—these are always the best.
2. A friend often makes a lot of jokes when you are trying to say something serious.
3. A friend keeps borrowing clothes or tapes without returning them.
4. A co-worker doesn't do his/her share of the work.
5. A teacher embarrasses you by criticizing you in front of your friends.

GROUP 19

Apologizing

Teenagers do not like to apologize. They think they will feel stupid or lose face. It is very difficult to recognize when you have done something wrong or hurt someone and even harder to then do something about it.

A sign of maturity is the ability to apologize. Although it may seem like this is a sign of weakness, it is actually a sign of strength. A person with self-confidence is capable of genuinely looking at the situation and apologizing *if it is justified*.

In this group session, we follow the same basic format as with Responding to Teasing and Resisting Peer Pressure in *The PRISM Workbook*. You practice apologizing using assertive body language and clear, assertive communication. The goal is to take responsibility for your actions—without taking "too much."

APOLOGIZING*

What Apologizing Means:

Apologizing means saying you're sorry for something you've said or done and *trying to make up for your mistake.*

Reasons to Apologize:

1. You may avoid being punished for your mistake.
2. You show that you take responsibility for your actions.
3. You may keep your friends' and others' trust in you.

When to Apologize:

1. Whenever you make a mistake.
2. When you hurt someone, make them angry, or break another person's things.
3. When you've broken a rule or promise.

Rules for Apologizing:

1. Only say what you really mean. Be honest.
2. Stay calm if the person does not accept your apology.

How to Apologize:

1. *Face* the person.
2. Make *eye contact.*
3. Use a *serious voice.*
4. Have a *serious face.*
5. Keep good *posture.*
6. *Ask* the person if you can *talk.*

*Adapted from J. B. Schumacher et al. (1988). *Social skills for daily living*, Circle Pines, MN: American Guidance Service.

7. *Say* you are *sorry*.
8. Say *what* you are sorry for doing.
9. *Tell your side.*
10. *Offer to change* if you can.
11. *Wait* for the person to accept your apology.
12. If the person accepts your apology, *say* you are *sorry* again and *change the subject*. If the person does *not* accept, say you are *sorry* again, *say* you will try to *change* and then *leave*.
13. *Positive self-talk.*

Role-Plays:

1. You break a promise to your parents to come home on time.
2. You acted without thinking and said something to a friend that hurt him or her.
3. You made a smart remark in class to your teacher.
4. You yelled at a staff member and got in trouble.

GROUP 20

Say What You Mean and Mean What You Say*
(aka A. J. and Brandon's Group)

This is an advanced group designed by two teenagers named A. J. and Brandon. They felt that with all the new skills they had learned in PRISM groups, there was still not a group that really helped them be assertive with their needs *and* take others' feelings into account at the same time.

They created the idea for this group and developed the steps. It is helpful in "sticky" situations when you have to tell someone something they might not want to hear, but if you didn't say it, it would hurt *you*. The purpose of the group is to help you learn how to communicate important things to others without hurting their feelings — and without overreacting to others' feelings, either.

First, you must define the problem and your goal. Next, you must decide what to say and the pros and cons of saying it. Then, you must figure out how the other person might feel hearing it (put yourself in their shoes). Finally, you state your message and don't give up even if the situation becomes difficult. As always, remember to use positive self-talk to help yourself feel good about what you've said.

*Thanks to Susan Lagasse, Ph.D., for collaborating on this technique.

GOAL

1. Be assertive.
2. Consider the other person's feelings.

STEPS

1. Define the problem and your goal.
2. Brainstorm ideas about what to say.
3. Talk about the *pros* and *cons* of each idea.
4. Think of how the other person will feel (put yourself in their shoes), but *don't overreact to the other person's feelings*.
5. Talk *assertively* and *appropriately*. Try to *respect* the *other persons's feelings*.
6. If the other person is hurt or angry, ask for advice from someone you trust about what to do.
7. Do not get discouraged. Use positive self-talk.
8. If possible, *try again. Don't give up*.

ROLE-PLAYS

1. Express your anger at your mother after she missed your baseball game but do *not* take her feelings into consideration.
2. Take your mother's feelings into consideration, but this time *overreact* to her feelings.
3. Follow the steps and try to be assertive to you mom while, at the same time, taking her feelings into consideration.

GROUP 21

The Five-Step Technique

The Five-Step Technique helps you stop and think before you make decisions.

It is important to learn these five basic questions to ask yourself before you do something. Actually, you ask four questions before, and then you ask another question afterwards.

If you can get in the habit of doing this, you will be surprised at how much better your judgment can be.

In this group session, we will start out by splitting into two teams and playing checkers. Each team uses The Five-Step Technique to make a decision about each move.

Then we move on to practicing social situations. Before you decide what to do or say in these role-plays, use the same steps that you did while playing checkers.

As you get better at this, you can apply it more and more in everyday situations.

1   What is the problem?

2   What are my choices?

3   What will happen if I choose. . . ?

4   Make a choice.

5   How did I do?

GROUP 22

How to Talk to Girls/Boys*

A few teenagers are very sophisticated or "street smart" and know how to make friends or initiate dates. Most teenagers, however, are not so sure. This group is designed to help you increase your confidence about making conversation and showing an interest in someone.

This is the kind of subject that many teenagers think about but rarely discuss. This is your chance to review and practice some of the basic steps to follow when you are interested in someone.

The self-talk that you use in these situations is just as important as what you actually say or do.

STEPS TO TALKING TO GIRLS/BOYS

After you have seen someone who you would like to talk to, you need to think about some things:

*Thanks to Jane Wells, Ph.D., for this technique.

First, Make a Decision

This means you need to decide what you want to accomplish in your first conversation. Do you just want to chat with the person? Do you want to get the person's phone number so that you can call him/her later on? Do you want to ask the person out on a date? No matter what your goal is, your nonverbal behavior should be the same: assertive, direct, and friendly. Once you've made your decision, you can begin with the following behavior steps.

Nonverbal Behaviors

1. Face the person.
2. Make eye contact.
3. Use a friendly tone of voice.
4. Smile!
5. Stay calm.

Talking

Of course, you'll want to do some talking along with your nonverbal behaviors—both to the other person as well as to yourself (your own silent self-talk). Here are hints to help you out:

1. Be interested in the person—ask them questions about themselves (where they go to school, what part of the city they live in, what they are doing at the moment).
2. Use Active Listening: Mirror and Clarify (see *The PRISM Workbook*).

    • "You sound _____ about _____." (Mirror)
              (feeling)   (situation)
    • "How did this happen?" (Clarify)

3. Use positive self-talk—no matter what happens.

Asking the Person Out

If you decide you want to ask the person out, some suggestions as to how to do that are below:

1. Find out if you have a common interest with the person. For example, maybe you both want to see the new Robin Williams movie. Or maybe you go to the same high school or like to hang out at the same mall.
2. If you do have things in common, you have two choices at this point:

   • You can ask the person specifically to go out right then.
   • You can ask the person for his/her phone number and call them up later to ask for a date.

If the Person Says "No"

If the person says "no," use the following steps:

1. Stay pleasant and use "Future Credit":

   • "Thanks anyway. Maybe some other time." (Future Credit)

2. Use positive self-talk for yourself:

   • "At least I tried."
   • "I handled that really well."
   • "I'm glad I spoke up; at least now I know. If I hadn't said anything, I would always be wondering."

If the Person Says "I do want to go out."

If the person says he/she does want to go out:

1. Be as specific as you can about a time to do so or when you'll arrange a time.
2. Write the phone number down — unless you've got a really good memory!

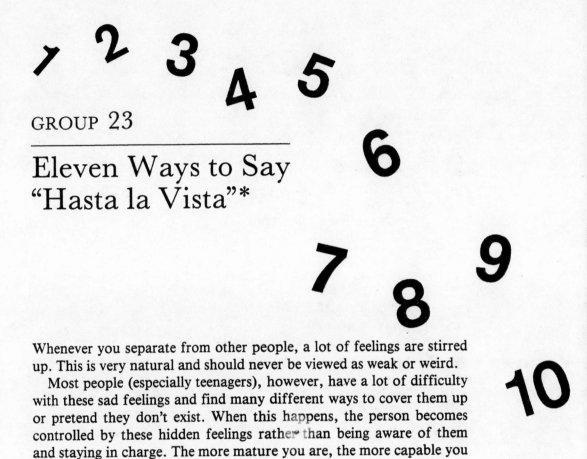

GROUP 23

Eleven Ways to Say "Hasta la Vista"*

Whenever you separate from other people, a lot of feelings are stirred up. This is very natural and should never be viewed as weak or weird.

Most people (especially teenagers), however, have a lot of difficulty with these sad feelings and find many different ways to cover them up or pretend they don't exist. When this happens, the person becomes controlled by these hidden feelings rather than being aware of them and staying in charge. The more mature you are, the more capable you are of recognizing and coping with these feelings.

In this session, we will review eleven typical ways that people deal with the emotions of separation. Each style has its own self-talk and behavior. After we discuss them, we will try a game known as "Hasta la Vista Charades." Each of you will act out one of the ways and see if you can get the rest of the group to guess which one it is.

*Thanks to Jane Wells, Ph.D., for collaborating on this technique.

"HASTA LA VISTA" STYLES

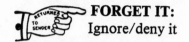 **FORGET IT:**
Ignore/deny it

Behaviors:

- Refusing to talk about leaving
- Won't answer questions about it
- Refusing to pack
- Won't say goodbye
- Won't use "Goodbye" book

Self-talk:

- "Leaving? What are you talking about?"
- "I don't remember when my discharge date is."
- "I forgot I was leaving."
- "I'm not leaving. Who told you that?"

ACT OUT:
Act out to stay

Behaviors:

- Pick fights with peers
- Act physically aggressive with staff/peers
- Verbally abuse people around you
- Destroy property

Self-talk:

- "I'll show them that I'm not ready to leave yet!"
- "I'm going to act out because I'm angry I have to leave."
- "Acting out is the only way to make them understand I'm not ready to leave."
- "Acting out? I'm not acting out!"

HATE THIS:

Hate this place, can't miss anybody, idealize other place

Behaviors:

- Complain a lot about how this place is horrible and the food is bad and about how ready you are to leave.
- Talk a lot about wherever it is you are going.
- Tell everyone how wonderful it is and how everyone there treats you much better than you are treated here.

Self-talk:

- "I can't wait to leave this pig sty!"
- "There's not one person here who I will miss after I leave."
- "The place I am going to is going to be absolutely perfect and I'm going to be 100% better just as soon as I leave here."

HATE THAT:

Increase sadness, devalue new place

Behaviors:

- Talk a lot about what an awful place it is that you are going to.
- Talk about what a wonderful, heavenly place this is.
- Sulk.
- Display "emotional" behaviors: being too sentimental, getting lost in your memories, spend all your time reminiscing about your life here.

Self-Talk:

- "This place has been wonderful to me and I just can't let it go."
- "No other place in the world can be as good as this one."
- "The only reason I have done so well here is because of the great staff and teachers. I'll never be able to find this anywhere else, and I'll never do as well anywhere else."

SPACE OUT:
Leave before you've left

Behaviors:

- Isolate: stop talking; stop participating in the program; refuse to participate in goodbye function; talk only about where you are going, and what you are going to do when you get there.

Self-talk:

- "I can't stand this place anymore . . . it makes me sick."
- "I don't want to be here anymore."
- "If I leave in my mind and just ignore everything here, then I don't have to feel the pain when I really do leave."

AWOL:
Taking off

Behaviors:

- AWOL before discharge

Self-talk:

- "I'll reject you before you reject me."
- "Fine! You want me to leave? Then I'll leave! And I'll make you feel guilty, too!"
- "If I AWOL, then they'll know I'm not ready to be discharged."

OBSESS:
Focus on leaving too much

Behaviors:

- Talking about leaving non-stop.
- Not talking about anything else.
- Writing about leaving; drawing pictures about leaving; saying goodbye to everybody daily.

Self-talk:

- "If I talk about it, then it won't hurt when I leave."
- "I'm really worried about leaving. If I talk about it constantly, then I don't really have to deal with it because I can just dump it in someone else's lap."
- "It makes me feel less anxious when I talk about it."
- "Unless I talk about it, I'm afraid people won't notice I'm leaving."

CLING:
Hang out at your program or school
after leaving and never let go

Behaviors:

- Continue to visit often, write letters to staff, peers and teachers; call everybody.
- Think about your program and the people here constantly after leaving.

Self-talk:

- "Nothing is as nice out in the world as it was while I was with you guys."
- "I'm afraid of failing out in the world. I'd rather stay where I feel safe."
- "I feel like a big fish in a small pond when I hang out here."

SHADES OF GRAY:

Combine the good with the bad
(the black with the white to make gray)

Behaviors:

- Making a list of the good things and the bad things here.
- Talking to a person here whom you have never liked and had trouble getting along with.
- Understanding that some things/people here have been helpful and some haven't been.

Self-talk:

- "This place is not all good, but it's not all bad either."
- "Some of my time there was really rough, but some of it was really good."
- "The people there are neither totally good nor totally bad; they are real people who are mixtures of both."

TEDDY BEAR:
Taking something of value with you

Behaviors:

- Getting your "Goodbye" book filled and taking it with you.
- Taking photographs of the friends you've made here
- Going over your memories in your head, enjoying them, and thinking of what you've learned.

- Enjoying talking to staff and peers about the funny things that have happened since you have been here. Talking about how far you have come since you first came here.
- Making something in Art Class to take with you that reminds you of this place.

Self-talk:

- "I'm going to take this with me and every time I look at it, I will remember thinking about my program or school and my experience there."
- "I'm going to keep this (object or memory) with me for a while to soothe me and calm me down whenever I feel stressed."

CONTRIBUTION:
Leaving something valuable behind—a legacy

Behaviors:

- Making something in Art Therapy or Art Class and leaving it for the unit.
- Writing about your experiences here and leaving it for a newcomer or having it published in a newsletter.

Self-talk:

- "Whenever I feel sad and miss this place, I can remember that something I made or did or contributed to this place is still living and may be helping someone else."
- "I know this place made a difference with me and it's nice to know that I made a difference here as well."